HOW EARTH'S LANDSCAPE AFFECTS THE WEATHER

ELIZABETH KRAJNIK

PowerKiDS press

NEW YORK

Published in 2019 by The Rosen Publishing Group, Inc.
29 East 21st Street, New York, NY 10010

Editor: Rachel Gintner
Cover Design: Michael Flynn
Interior Layout: Rachel Rising

Photo Credits: Cover FiledIMAGE/Shutterstock.com; Cover, pp. 3, 4, 6, 7, 8, 10, 11, 12, 14, 15, 16, 18, 19, 20, 21, 22, 23, 24 (background) chaowat kawera/Shutterstock.com; p. 5 CroMary/Shutterstock.com; p. 6 randy andy/Shutterstock.com; p. 7 Designua/Shutterstock.com; p. 9 Volodymyr Burdiak/Shutterstock.com; pp. 10, 14,17, 19 Courtesy of NASA Image and Video Library; p. 11 Gary Wiepert/ASSOCIATED PRESS/Alamy Stock Photo; p. 13 Pavliha/E+/Getty Images; p. 15 DigitalPen/Shutterstock.com; p. 20 Li Hui Chen/Shutterstock.com; p. 21 evenfh/Shutterstock.com; p. 22 Kues/Shutterstock.com.

Cataloging-in-Publication Data

Names: Krajnik, Elizabeth.
Title: How Earth's landscape affects the weather / Elizabeth Krajnik.
Description: New York : PowerKids Press, 2019. | Series: Spotlight on weather and natural disasters | Includes glossary and index.
Identifiers: LCCN ISBN 9781508169031 (pbk.) | ISBN 9781508169017 (library bound) | ISBN 9781508169048 (6 pack)
Subjects: LCSH: Weather--Juvenile literature. | Landscapes--Juvenile literature. | Landscape changes--Juvenile literature.
Classification: LCC QC981.3 K73 2019 | DDC 551.5--dc23

Manufactured in the United States of America

CPSIA Compliance Information: Batch #CS18PK For further information contact Rosen Publishing, New York, New York at 1-800-237-9932.

CONTENTS

CHAPTER ONE

WHAT WE SEE

Earth's landscape is made up of many different landforms. Take a look outside. What do you see? You might see a mountain range or a thick forest. These are just two kinds of landscapes—there are many others on Earth.

What some people may not realize is that Earth's different landscapes affect the weather. People living on one side of a mountain might experience a large amount of **precipitation** throughout the year, while people living on the other side of the mountain might have much drier weather. People living near a forest might experience multiple kinds of weather, such as rain, snow, or **droughts**.

We base some of our daily decisions, such as our choice of clothing, on the weather. We also make much larger decisions, such as where to plant crops, based on the climate in an area.

Some people choose their clothes for the day based on the weather. If it's raining, you'll probably wear a raincoat and carry an umbrella. These boys might live near a forest in the Pacific Northwest where it rains a lot.

CHAPTER TWO

EARTH'S OCEANS

If we look at a picture of Earth taken from outer space, we can see that much of Earth's surface—more than 70 percent—is covered by oceans. Because water covers such a large portion of Earth, it has a large effect on global weather. An El Niño climate **cycle** occurs in part when warm water in the western **tropical** Pacific Ocean travels east along the **equator** and arrives near the northwestern coast of South America. This climate cycle can lead to increased ocean temperatures and changes in Earth's atmosphere.

El Niños usually don't occur every year. They can happen as often as every two years or as infrequently as every seven years. An El Niño can last from nine to twelve months.

THE EL NIÑO CYCLE

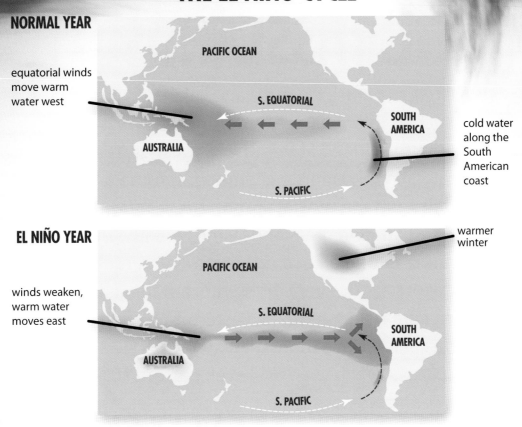

NORMAL YEAR

PACIFIC OCEAN

equatorial winds move warm water west

S. EQUATORIAL

SOUTH AMERICA

cold water along the South American coast

AUSTRALIA

S. PACIFIC

EL NIÑO YEAR

warmer winter

PACIFIC OCEAN

winds weaken, warm water moves east

S. EQUATORIAL

SOUTH AMERICA

AUSTRALIA

S. PACIFIC

When changes occur in Earth's atmosphere, different weather patterns happen. During an El Niño climate cycle, tropical storms move eastward with the moving ocean water. This can lead to more precipitation on the western shores of South America and hurricanes in the Pacific Ocean. However, El Niño events cause changes in weather all over the world.

CHAPTER THREE

GRASSLANDS

Different names for grasslands are used around the world, such as "pampas" in South America and "savannas" in Africa. In the United States, the biggest grassland is the Great Plains, a region that stretches from Canada to Mexico through the central part of the country.

The weather in grasslands varies greatly. The temperature of one area of the Great Plains, such as North Dakota, can be very different from the temperature in another area, such as Texas. Eastern Texas and Oklahoma can receive more than 50 inches (127 cm) of precipitation each year. However, parts of Montana, Wyoming, and western Texas may receive less than 15 inches (38.1 cm) of precipitation each year.

Tornadoes, which are whirling windstorms with funnel-shaped clouds, are more likely to form in the central part of the Great Plains. This is because warm, moist air from the Gulf of Mexico meets cold, dry air from Canada, causing the air to rotate.

The African savanna is a tropical grassland. Tropical grasslands generally experience a dry season and a rainy season. They have warm temperatures year-round. **Temperate** grasslands have a growing season and a **dormant** season, when grass can't grow because the temperature is too cold.

CHAPTER FOUR

THE GREAT LAKES

The Great Lakes are a very special feature of the United States and the world. These large bodies of freshwater affect the weather in the northeastern part of the United States, and the people living near them have learned to adapt. During different seasons, the Great Lakes act as a heat sink or a heat source. A heat sink is something that absorbs, or takes in, more heat than it gives off. A heat source is something that radiates, or gives off, more heat than it absorbs.

THE GREAT LAKES DURING HEAVY SNOW

Lake-effect snow forms when lake water is warm and the air is cold. The lake water **evaporates** into the air and warms it. The warm air rises higher into the atmosphere and cools. Clouds form, and, if it's cold enough, snow may fall.

This photograph from November 2014 shows a wall of lake-effect snow crossing Lake Erie and approaching the city of Buffalo, New York.

In the summer, air temperatures near the lakes are cooler than inland temperatures. The water absorbs the heat near the shores slowly and holds on to it for a long time. The Great Lakes act as a heat sink in the summer and a heat source in the winter.

CHAPTER FIVE

DESERTS

Most people think of deserts as hot places. However, deserts also experience cold temperatures. A desert is a place where there's little to no precipitation. Earth has five kinds of deserts: subtropical, coastal, rain shadow, interior, and polar.

The world's largest subtropical desert is the Sahara in northern Africa. These deserts form because of the movements of air masses. Near the equator, hot, moist air rises. As the air rises, it cools and gives off its moisture in the form of heavy rains. The air mass, which is now cool and dry, moves away from the equator, gets closer to the ground, and warms. As the air moves lower, it keeps clouds from forming. As a result, very little rain occurs in these areas.

Even though rain rarely occurs in deserts, flash floods happen from time to time. Sudden thunderstorms can cause these fast-moving floods, which are powerful and can destroy things in their path.

A sandstorm occurs when strong winds in sandy areas, such as some deserts, pick up loose sand and blow it all over the place. These storms can create very low visibility. Sands blown from the Sahara can cause dark skies throughout Europe.

CHAPTER SIX

MOUNTAINS

If you live on one side of a mountain, the weather you experience will likely be much different than the weather on the other side of the mountain. A mountain forces air approaching it to rise. Clouds form and then let out precipitation. This is called the orographic effect, and it happens on the **windward** side of a mountain. On the **leeward** side of the mountain, the drier air descends and warms. The windward side of the mountain is more temperate and has more plants, while the leeward side of the mountain is drier and hotter.

The Himalayas keep moisture from reaching the Tibetan Plateau, creating a great example of a rain shadow desert.

OROGRAPHIC PRECIPITATION

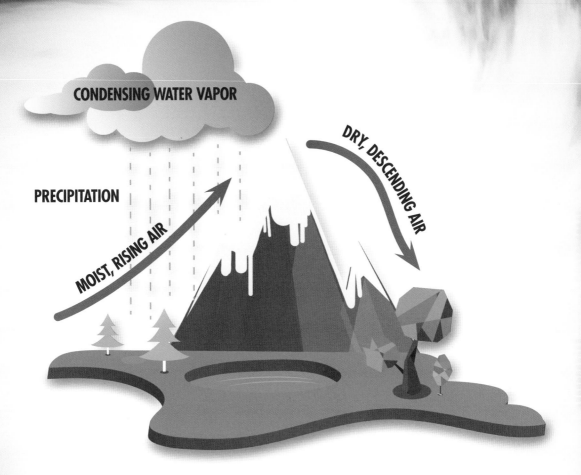

CONDENSING WATER VAPOR

PRECIPITATION

MOIST, RISING AIR

DRY, DESCENDING AIR

Places with these drier, hotter conditions are known as rain shadow deserts. In the United States, the Sierra Nevada mountain range creates a rain shadow desert. This desert, which is the lowest, driest place in North America, is called Death Valley.

CHAPTER SEVEN

FORESTS

Forests cover about 30 percent of Earth. Trees take in carbon dioxide, a gas that can be harmful to people and Earth, and produce the oxygen we need to breathe. Trees also affect the weather because they release moisture into the atmosphere. Their leaves help keep the air on Earth at a cool temperature. Through a process called evapotranspiration, the combined processes of evaporation and **transpiration**, trees change water from a liquid to a gas.

Some studies show that planting trees in an area where there were no trees before can increase precipitation. The opposite is also true: deforestation can decrease precipitation because there's less moisture released.

Over time, trees can change the climate because they reduce the amount of carbon dioxide in the atmosphere. However, if deforestation continues, the climate will change in a harmful way.

Countries have different laws about deforestation practices. This **satellite** image shows that there's more forested land in Belize (right) than there is in Guatemala (left).

CHAPTER EIGHT

CITIES

Even though cities are human-made parts of Earth's landscape, they do affect the weather. As people construct cities, plants are lost to roads, buildings, and other structures. With fewer trees, cities have less shade to lower surface temperatures. Trees reduce air temperatures through evapotranspiration—therefore fewer trees means that water in cities evaporates quickly. This leaves the area warmer and drier than before. Areas where this occurs are called heat islands.

Heat islands can exist on the surface and in the atmosphere. Surface heat islands occur when the sun heats surfaces, such as roofs and things made of cement, to temperatures much higher than the air. Atmospheric heat islands occur when the temperature of the air surrounding a city is higher than the air in the areas near the city. Communities can address these issues by planting trees and other plants near buildings.

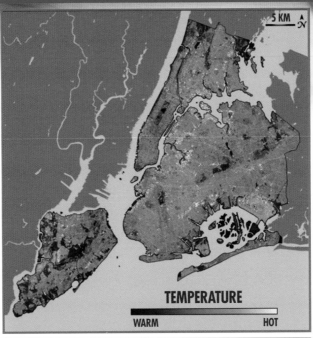

TEMPERATURE

WARM   HOT

5 KM

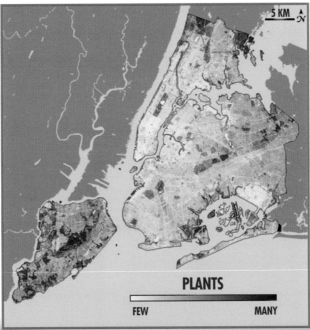

PLANTS

FEW   MANY

5 KM

These satellite images show temperatures (top) and plants (bottom) around New York City. When we compare the two, we can see that areas with more plants are cooler and areas with fewer plants are hotter.

CHAPTER NINE

THE POLES

Weather in the polar regions is affected by their position on Earth, their elevation, and how much land each region has. The Arctic region, which is centered on the North Pole, is made up mostly of the Arctic Ocean. The ocean keeps the Arctic region warmer than Antarctica, which is the continent at the South Pole. Because Antarctica is a landmass, there's no ocean under it to keep it warm. The Arctic region also stays warmer because it's at sea level. As elevation increases, temperature decreases. The elevation of Antarctica is an average 1.43 miles (2.3 km) above sea level.

Albedo is the fraction of sunlight that a surface reflects back into outer space. Ice has a high albedo value, and thus, helps keep Earth cool. However, as ice melts into water, which has a lower albedo value, more of the sun's energy is absorbed and Earth warms.

The freezing temperatures in the Arctic and Antarctic regions create polar deserts in these areas. In fact, almost the entire continent of Antarctica is a polar desert. The area experiences little to no precipitation and is very cold.

CHAPTER TEN

WEATHER OUTLOOK

The weather of our landscapes may change in the coming years. Right now, Earth is experiencing climate change. In the United States alone, **extreme** temperatures are occurring more often than ever before. Our summers are hotter and our winters are warmer. We're experiencing more precipitation and precipitation-related events. Scientists believe these changes in weather and climate are caused by humans.

We have the power to turn around the effects of climate change by understanding that it's a problem and then taking steps to solve this problem quickly. One way people can try to undo the harm we've caused is by planting more trees and plants in cities. This will help fix surface and atmospheric heat islands. It will also help decrease the amount of carbon dioxide in the air. What else can you do to save Earth?

GLOSSARY

cycle (SYH-kuhl) A series of events that, once complete, repeats itself.

dormant (DOHR-muhnt) Not active but able to become active.

drought (DROHWT) A period of time during which there is very little or no rain.

equator (ih-KWAY-tuhr) A circle around Earth that is equally distant from the North Pole and South Pole.

evaporate (ih-VAH-puh-rayt) To change from a liquid into a gas.

extreme (ihk-STREEM) Very great in degree.

leeward (LEE-wurd) A side of something that is away from the wind.

precipitation (prih-sih-puh-TAY-shuhn) Water that falls to the ground as hail, mist, rain, sleet, or snow.

satellite (SAA-tuh-lyt) A spacecraft placed in orbit around Earth, a moon, or a planet to collect information or for communication.

temperate (TEM-puh-ruht) Not too hot or too cold.

transpiration (trans-puh-RAY-shuhn) The process by which plants give off water vapor through openings in their leaves.

tropical (TRAH-pih-kuhl) Of or relating to the tropics, usually having to do with warm, wet weather.

windward (WIND-wurd) A side of something that faces the wind.

INDEX

PRIMARY SOURCE LIST

Page 14
Composite satellite image of the Himalayan range. Photograph. Taken by the International Space Station. December 27, 2017. Courtesy of NASA.

Page 17
Belize-Guatemala border. Photograph. Taken by the NASA Terra satellite. May 10, 2016. Courtesy of NASA.

Page 19
Maps of New York temperature and vegetation. Created by Robert Simmon using data from the NASA/USGS Landsat satellite. August 2, 2006. Courtesy of NASA.

WEBSITES